Terrifyingly Talented

by

Andy Winters

First published in Great Britain in 2010
by Caboodle Books Ltd
Copyright © Andy Winters 2010

A Catalogue record for this book is available
from the British Library.

ISBN 978-0-9565239-0-7

Illustrations and front cover by Al Jacques
Page Layout by Highlight Type Bureau Ltd
Printed by Cox and Wyman

The paper and board used in the paperback by
Caboodle Books Ltd are natural recyclable products
made from wood grown in sustainable forests.
The manufacturing processes conform to the environmental
regulations of the country of origin.

Caboodle Books Ltd
Riversdale, 8 Rivock Avenue, Steeton, BD20 6SA
www.authorsabroad.com

CONTENTS

For Rory, Kate and Jack

WARNING

If you turn this page you might find that you will not be able to put this book down. I cannot accept responsibility for you being late for school, missing your dental appointment or missing a shopping trip with grandma. (Ok I'll accept responsibility for the last one) All the characters portrayed in this book are entirely real. All the events actually happened. Only continue if you are prepared to laugh out loud and gasp in astonishment. Please make sure that you are with a friend, have access to the internet or you at least have a mobile phone to hand, as you will find yourself desperate to pass on all the unbelievable facts that you are about to learn.

The Seven Amazing Acts waiting to be unleashed from these pages will astound and astonish you, amaze and confound you. You will believe that the impossible is possible.

Do not attempt any of the tricks or stunts which appear in this book. (Oh hang on a minute, except for the three at the end. They are just for you!)

DANGER

This book could change your life

Terrifyingly Talented

ARTistes FARTistes and FUNambulists

The flimsy rope stretches across the full width of the Niagara River. Above is a blinding blue sky, 50m below is a swirling torrent of violent river water which has just spewed and spat its way over the magnificent Niagara Falls.

Along the banks of the river over 100,000 spectators line up, amongst them, The Prince of Wales. A passenger boat 'The Maid of the Mist' sails beneath the rope, its decks weighed down by sightseeing passengers, all of them squinting up at the thin line above.

Suddenly a lone figure appears at the top of the gorge. The crowd falls silent, giving way to the thunderous roar of the river. The date is the 14th September 1860 and the lone figure is Frenchman, Charles Blondin. He is about to attempt to cross the river using a tightrope. (Yes that's right, he is going to walk along a thin rope, high above a rocky river) Just in case the spectators don't think that he is totally insane, he is also going to attempt this daring feat wearing stilts. (You can find out how he gets on in Act 6.)

This is just one of the many ways in which people got their entertainment before the advent of radio, television, cinema, computers and games consoles. Believe it or not, there actually was a time before entertainment was beamed into your house via the telly, ask your grandma. (But be careful, on hearing this question, grandma may give you a clip around the ears!)

Today we have TV shows such as 'Britain's Got Talent' or 'America's Got Talent'. They showcase a variety of acts. It's difficult not to enjoy watching Simon Cowell give his opinion on the hundreds of performers that all want to make it to the big time. Most of these acts are called 'live' acts because they perform in front of a 'live' audience in theatres, clubs and holiday camps. (I suppose performing in front of a dead audience might be a bit strange if not a bit smelly. At least you wouldn't get booed off.) Anyway, Simon and his fellow panellists can make or break an act. TV is a very good way for an act to get seen by millions of people in one go. One good TV performance can secure lots of theatre bookings. One poor performance could be the end of the act.

Before TV came along, reputations were earned on the Music Hall circuit.

Our Victorian ancestors would often enjoy a night out at the Theatre or Music Halls, where they would be entertained by: singers; actors; acrobats; jugglers; strongmen; sword swallowers; fire eaters; comedians; magicians; animals; human cannonballs and funambulists (that's tightrope walkers to you) Yes, Charles Blondin was a funambulist , it doesn't sound like much fun to me. Why didn't he just use a bridge like everybody else?

The first superstar of Music Hall was called S. Cowell (Sam) He was a great comedian and singer and toured Theatres across Europe and USA. I wonder if he would have met with S Cowell's (Simons) approval.

All these acts would appear on the same night. This was called a Bill. The acts would be advertised on a poster which was a bit like a menu of entertainment. The best acts were at the top of the bill and the up and coming acts were at the bottom. The ones at the top were the Stars of the Show. The ones at the bottom were known as the Wines and Spirits, because their names were usually in smaller print than the refreshment prices. The evening's entertainment was overseen and introduced by the Chairman of the Hall or Master of Ceremonies, otherwise referred to as the MC.

THE HIPPODROME

Appearing Twice Nightly

A REALLY GOOD SINGER

A BRILLIANT MAGICIAN

A WELL LOVED COMEDIAN

AN AMAZING ACROBAT

An Ok Singer

A Magician

A Funnyman

An Acrobat

Somebody whose Mum said they could sing
A bloke who got a magic set for Christmas
A man whose mates say he's funny
A woman doing roly polys

Other Victorian entertainment

Public executions: You could buy tickets for a hanging. You would have to queue early because crowds of thousands would gather. There would even be people selling refreshments and souvenirs.

Thanks Mum.
It's just what I've
always wanted!

Laughing gas: People would volunteer to go up on stage and be administered a lung full of Nitrous Oxide (The sort of stuff they give to mums during childbirth) Then the audience would watch the victims, (I mean volunteers) go totally bonkers.

Ratting: *Two dogs (two very hungry and vicious dogs) were thrown into a sunken pit. The local rat catcher would then empty a sack of rats into the pit. Spectators would take bets on how many rats were killed. Sometimes up to 200 rats would be killed in one session. ... Rat's entertainment.....*

This is not very sportsman like!

Cock fighting: *Two cockerels would slug it out in a cockpit. Our Victorian ancestors took bets on which cock would survive the gruelling contest. The cockpit was a very small area; hence a pilot's cabin is known as a cockpit.*

Travelling Shows: *There would be circuses and other shows which would roll into town and settle on parkland. These shows would often bring curiosities such as the world's tallest or shortest man, (See Act 7) a two headed goat, or a bearded lady (don't ask your grandma)*

Ok so let's travel back to the Victorian era. We'll go to the local Music Hall. Music Halls were often very grand buildings with beautiful stone masonry on the outside. They would have exotic names such as the Adelphi, Alhambra, Hippodrome, Phoenix, Empire, Egyptian Hall, Gaiety, Parthenon and Coliseum. (Check out if there was or still is one in your area.)

These exotic names were imported from the far flung countries of the British Empire. Architects would recreate the designs of Greek and Egyptian buildings when constructing new Music Halls. Legend has it that an American business man bought thousands of Egyptian Mummies and used their bandages to make paper. Some of the paper was used to make theatre programmes.

Yes it's a nice building but it doesn't *really* quite fit in !

The interiors of the Music Halls were plush; they would often have seating for over two thousand customers. The floors were laid with thick carpets and the walls were lined with designer paper. Intricate plasterwork covered the ceilings. Whilst gas lighting lit up the stage.

Theatres were real fire hazards. Many Victorian theatres burnt down. On 30th December 1903 the Iroquois Theatre in Chicago burnt down during a performance killing 575 people.

There was often a rowdy atmosphere. Oranges were a popular refreshment. Lots of alcohol was consumed on the night and many of the audience smoked pipes. People of all ages attended, even mothers with babies. Oh yes, there were also the Mashers and the Scuttlers.

MASHERS: *The fashionable men about town. The Mashers were wealthy City gents, solicitors, doctors and industrialists. They wore tailored suits and because of their aloof attitude towards the working classes they were often lampooned by songwriters. These songs became very popular on the Music Hall circuit. I suppose it's a bit like today's comedians making fun of politicians and celebrities.*

SCUTTLERS: *Gangs of young people. They wore clogs with sharp brass tips on them. They also wore their caps back to front with what they called a donkey fringe sticking out. Bell bottom trousers were kept in place by a heavy duty brass buckled belt. This not only kept their trousers up it also acted as a weapon when a fight broke out, which it often did. Scuttlers would sometimes loiter outside Music Halls and commit an offence known as bonneting. They would grab the hats off a Mashers good lady companion and then tread it into the ground. (For Scuttler think Chav.)*

Ok, so you've decided that you don't want to hang around for the Public Execution. Ratting is cruel to dogs and even crueller to rats. You've been woken up so many times at 5am by cockerels crowing that you just couldn't care less if two of them want to fight it out and the local park already has more than its fair share of curiosities. Instead, you've settled for the Music Hall.

Ladies and Gentlemen, boys and girls, chavs and chavnots, you've made the right choice. For your pleasure please take a seat and read on. I have engaged some of the most daring and dangerous, bravest and brilliant maddest and baddest, death defying acts that ever appeared on the boards (that's the stage to you) of British Music Hall. Any one of them might have appeared in your town or city. We know that Britain's got Talent here is the proof that

BRITAIN HAD TALENT.

APPEARING INSIDE

IN NO PARTICULAR ORDER

Marvel at one of the greatest magicians that ever lived
(and died)
CHUNG LING SOO

Hold your breath (and your nose) and take a
ringside seat for the amazing
LE PETOMANE.

Saddle up for **BUFFALO BILLS**
Wild West Extravaganza

Be Afraid, be very afraid of **LA FAYETTE**. He's the highest
paid illusionist of his day. He's also the strangest.

Watch the impossible become possible at the hands of
the most famous Escape Artiste the world has ever seen,
HARRY HOUDINI.

Gaze in awe at The Hero of Niagara, the one and only
CHARLES BLONDIN.

And finally, please give a Jumbo sized welcome for
P T BARNUM's Greatest Show on Earth.

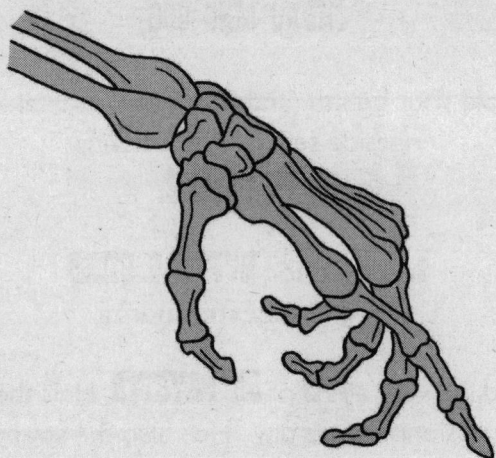

ACT ONE

CHUNG LING SOO

1861- 1918

THE MAN OF MYSTERY

Chung Ling Soo, 'The Original Chinese Conjuror', astounded audiences across the globe with his extravagant stage shows. He wore traditional Chinese silk costumes embroidered with gold. His stage props were crafted to the highest standards and were decorated with Chinese dragons and flames using vivid colours which would give the show an exotic feel. He spoke only Chinese and he would always have an interpreter by his side.

Chung Ling Soo was inspired by another Oriental magician named Ching Ling Foo who was arguably the more talented illusionist. Ling Foo could produce a 4 metre pole from his mouth and then from nowhere he would produce a bowl of water from which he then produced a small child (a very wet small child).

Why didn't I just get a paper round?

It was after seeing Ling Foo perform that Ling Soo decided to embark on his spectacular Chinese stage show. At one point both magicians were performing in theatres in London just 100 metres apart. Some say that they had a bitter rivalry others claim that the rivalry was just a publicity stunt which suited them both. Either way it resulted in Ling Foo challenging Ling Soo to a sort of magic show duel. Ling Foo said that he would give Ling Soo £1000 if he could do 10 out of 20 of his tricks.

Ling Soo accepted the challenge; however when he turned up to the theatre with all the press waiting to record the event, Ling Foo failed to show. Ling Soo, with the help of his interpreter, declared himself the winner. The press and the public agreed. This propelled Ling Soo to even greater fame and his show became even more popular.

But like most magicians and conjurors, Ling Soo enjoyed the dark and dangerous side of magic. He also kept a well guarded secret. His desire for danger and fame would end his career at the Wood Green Empire Theatre in London. It would also reveal his long held secret.

Chung Ling Soo had started to do one of magic's most dangerous stunts. The 'Catching a Bullet Trick'. Let's face it, we all like watching danger. It gets our adrenalin going. A formula one racing crash or a bruising football challenge has more appeal than a boring non event (or is that just me) Oh well, Ling Soo would get members of the audience to mark two bullets. Sometimes he would catch them in his teeth and spit them out onto a plate. At other performances he would catch the bullets with his bare hands and throw them onto the plate.

On the fateful night at Wood Green Empire, Ling Soo was performing to a packed audience. Two of his Chinese assistants aimed their rifles at Ling Soo's chest. The audience gripped their seats in anticipation. The smell of Chinese incense, and pipe tobacco swirled around the auditorium. Ling Soo stared down the barrels of both rifles confident that he would suffer no harm as he had secretly palmed the bullets into his hand during the loading of the guns.

The assistants pulled the triggers, the sweet smell of gunpowder now mingled in with the incense and tobacco. Little swirls of blue smoke danced out of the gun. The audience breathed in the tense atmosphere waiting for Ling Soo to spit out the bullets. Instead he dropped to the stage floor. The audience screamed as they realised that the trick had gone terribly wrong. Almost immediately Ling Soo uttered his last words.

'Oh my god. Something's happened.

Lower the curtain'.

Butter Fingers!

Ling Soo died the following day. One of the guns had not been cleaned properly and a stray bullet had passed clean through his chest.

Some of the witnesses were more surprised by Ling Soo's last words than by the accident. Ling Soo had always said that he could not speak English. However, his death revealed that he had never even stepped foot in China. He was in fact Scots/American born William Ellsworth Robinson who had painstakingly disguised himself as a Chinese conjurer. He had previously been billed as 'Robinson Man of Mystery'.

Robinson had fooled lots of people. He had maintained the Chinese character of Chung Ling Soo for many years and he gave great pleasure to his audience. William Ellsworth Robinson was indeed a man of mystery.

R.I.P.

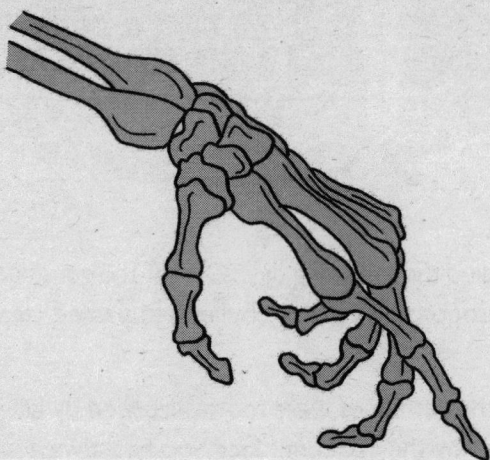

ACT TWO

LE PETOMANE

1857 -1945

The Moulin Rouge is the greatest Music Hall in Paris. Tonight's top of the bill is Le Petomane. The Hall is filled to capacity. The heavy stench of cigarette smoke, oranges and perfume fills the air. The audience sits silently, awaiting the highest paid entertainer in the whole of France.

An expectant murmur wafts around the auditorium. Suddenly, the gas lights dim, and two huge blue velvet curtains rise slowly to reveal tonight's main attraction.

Le Petomane walks elegantly towards centre stage. He is a tall handsome man dressed in black dinner jacket, red tailor made trousers and white silk gloves. He is sporting a large moustache and sweptback dark hair.

Le Petomane will treat tonight's sell out crowd to an evening of songs and impressions. Only he will do it differently, very differently, very differently indeed.

Le Petomane will not sing from his mouth, instead he will use his backside. For, translated into English, Le Petomane means Fartiste.

The audience scream with laughter as he shows off his range of alto, tenor, bass and baritone blasts.

First, Le Petomane recreates the sound of cannon fire and thunderstorms. Next he makes the sound of a piece of cloth being ripped for a full ten seconds (so now you know where the saying 'let rip' comes from) Mimicking the sound of a bumble bee and pretending to catch it is always a real crowd pleaser. He will lie down on the floor and blow out candles. Just to show off, he will place a rubber tube up his bum and attach a musical instrument called an ocarina, he will then treat the audience to a medley of popular tunes. For his finale he will blast his way through an impression of an earthquake.

Audiences across Europe went wild for Le Petomane, who could command up to 20,000 Francs per show. (I don't know, but it's a lot of money) So how did he learn his trade and was it just Music Hall trickery?

Le Petomane was born Joseph Pujol in Marseilles France on June 1st 1857. He left school at the age of 14 and became an apprentice baker. At weekends Joseph would go to the beach with friends and swim in the warm blue waters of the Mediterranean. It was whilst swimming that he discovered his hidden talent. Joseph stood up in the water and took in a huge breath. At the same time his backside sucked up a large amount of seawater. Joseph screamed with shock (well you would wouldn't you?) He ran out of the sea with jets of water shooting out of his bathing costume. His distress was so great that his mum took him to the doctors. The doctor put him at his ease and explained to Joseph that he had a rare medical condition which enabled him to suck in air or water though his bottom.(It probably doesn't get much rarer than that)

The good news is that the condition is not life threatening. The bad news is your son just can't stop farting!

Joseph was already a natural showman and performer, he would regularly sing at home when guests came around and he was also a talented musician.

It was during a stint in the French army when Joseph realised that his rare gift could be used for entertainment. He told one of his fellow soldiers about his experience in the sea and was immediately handed a bucket of water and told to 'prove it'. Within minutes Joseph had created a man made fountain.

His friends fell to the floor with laughter. They christened him Le Petomane, The Fartiste. Joseph's career was born.

He left behind him a life of baking bread and instead took up a career in breaking wind. Joseph's act quickly gained a good reputation with audiences in the South of France. This gave him the confidence to approach the owner of the Moulin Rouge. Joseph arrived unannounced and after demonstrating his skills he was booked on the spot to perform that very same evening.

Audiences took to Le Petomane immediately. He had a great stage presence and delivered his act in a deadpan manner. (He didn't take himself too seriously) His true personality also shone through for Joseph was well loved by friends and family (He had ten children) It was by helping a friend that he lost his job at the Moulin Rouge. Joseph knew somebody who sold cakes and biscuits on a market stall. To help him drum up business, Joseph would often go to the stall and give free performances. The owner of the Moulin Rouge got wind of this (well he would, wouldn't he)and he ordered Joseph to stop, however, he always put family and friends first.

He left the Moulin Rouge and started his own travelling theatre show called The Theatre Pompadour. He eventually retired. Joseph wanted to spend time with his family. Three of his sons were seriously injured in battle during the First World War. The horror and devastation of the conflict had a profound effect on him. He gave up the theatre and along with his family he went back into business as a baker. Joseph died at the ripe old age of 88.

Apparently if you hear a strange noise in the theatre it might be the ghost of Le Petomane. (Well you've got to blame someone)

Did you know that years ago in Ireland there were professional fartistes called 'braigetori'

The Japanese had fart dancers called Oribe

Paul Oldfield from Macclesfield, England, is a professional fartiste who goes under the stage name of Mr Methane.

King Henry II had a court jester called Roland the Farter. Each Christmas the King held a party and Roland would perform a routine called 'one jump, one whistle and one fart'.

Do you think you could do something a little different this year?

How about one jump, one whistle and two farts?

ACT THREE
BUFFALO BILLS WILD
WEST CONGRESS OF
ROUGH RIDERS
OF THE WORLD

Dozens of Tepees (Wigwams or tents) line the banks of the icy river. 97 Native Americans from the Oglala tribe of the Sioux Nation sit around camp fires recounting tales of the bloody battles they fought alongside Chief Sitting Bull. Many of them had fought at the Battle of Little Big Horn where General George Armstrong Custer and 268 of his men were slaughtered. (Not to be confused with General Custard who was defeated at the annual flan flinging convention)

Some of the young braves are tending to the horses. The children run around laughing and chasing one another, their hot breath turning into little puffs of steam as it meets the freezing air. Suddenly one of the Sioux braves stands up.

His name is 'Surrounded' He is 6ft 7ins tall dressed in a shirt and leggings made of deer skin, (Q. What do you call a 6ft 7in Native American Warrior? A. Anything he tells you to call him) on his feet are a pair of leather moccasins and hanging from his belt is a knife in a sheath and a small bag of face paint. A huge buffalo skin robe is fending off the cold. He turns to the medicine man, 'Black Elk' who is wearing a feather headdress constructed from Eagle feathers and horsehair. 'Surrounded' is hungry. It is time to venture out of the camp and get food. Another brave, 'Charging Thunder' grabs his buffalo skin robe and the three of them set off.

However, hunting wild beasts is not what they have in mind. Today the Sioux are going into the Industrial heartland of

Salford Nr Manchester. They are going down to the local pub for a pint of beer and a good old Lancashire Hot Pot. (Yes really... I know it's hard to believe ...Just bear with me and I'll explain). The Tepees are lined up on the banks of the River Irwell in Salford and the Sioux are part of Buffalo Bills Wild West Show.

The show took up five acres of Land at Salford Quays. If you ever go to the Lowry Centre then you are standing on the exact spot where the Sioux and other warriors from around the world recreated mock battles and performed stunts to audiences for an amazing five month stint.

The ring master and creator of the show was William Fredrick Cody, known as 'Buffalo Bill' He picked up the name by selling Buffalo meat to American Railroad engineers. Bill would often tell stories about his exploits in the Wild West regions of America. He soon realised that people in cities such as New York and London were very interested in the Wild West.

The Wild West was not really as wild as it seemed. Cowboys were outnumbered by thousands to one by farmers. In fact some towns were so keen to keep up a bad reputation for gun slinging and bar brawling that they would stage mock fights using actors each time a train pulled into the station.

Bill recruited famous names such as Chief Sitting Bull, along with two of America's most famous sharp shooters, Annie Oakley (Portrayed in the film 'Annie Get your Gun') and notorious gun slinger, Wild Bill Hickok.   The shows became very popular and soon Bill was a very wealthy man. He would never sell another buffalo steak again. Not that he could if he'd wanted to, the European settlers in America virtually wiped out the Buffalo population. The numbers went from a whopping 30 million down to a measly one hundred. Instead he ploughed his money back into the Show and '**Buffalo Bills Wild West Congress of Rough Riders of the World'** was born.

Bill and his 200 strong company of performers comprising of, Sioux, Mexican, Japanese, Cossack and Arab horsemen, set sail for England in 1897. Oh yes and on top of the 200 people, he also brought 180 horses and 18 buffalo. (Make that 82 remaining buffalo)

This was a truly amazing experience for the natives of Manchester. They had read books about the Wild West and the invention of cinemas in 1895 had enabled them to see moving pictures of America for the first time. England was ready for Buffalo Bill and all his shows were played to huge crowds.

A typical Wild West show

On entry to the show, people could walk around the Sioux camp and see how a typical Native American family would live.

This was a sort of 'Human Zoo' which was another popular crowd pleaser in Victorian times. Unfortunately many exhibits (human beings) in 'human zoos' were exploited and displayed as 'primitive people' or as 'freak shows'.

Bill cared dearly for the Oglala Sioux and he wanted to show the human side of them rather than the aggressive side which was portrayed in the newspapers and films. (The 1990 film 'Dancing With Wolves' is a portrayal of the Oglala tribe)

Once the show started, Bill would show off his shooting skills. Whilst riding a horse at full gallop he would shoot objects which were thrown up into the air by his assistants.

The Mexicans would give a display of their lasso skills and the other nationalities would demonstrate their own particular horse riding methods.   Japanese jugglers and acrobats would summersault their way around the arena, and then mock battles would follow. The grand finale would be 'Custer's Last Stand' with Bill playing Custer.

However the star of the show turned out to be a young cowboy named Carter, 'The Cowboy Cyclist'. Carter would ride down a steep ramp on a bicycle and jump a distance of 56feet.

Carter's act was certainly the audience's favourite. Bikes were a lot cheaper to maintain and keep than horses. So Carter proved that huge travelling shows did not need to rely on live animals.

Buffalo Bill was a great entrepreneur. He toured his show around Europe and eventually settled back in America where he bought hotels, ranches and lots and lots of land. He died of Kidney failure in 1917.

But what happened to the three Oglala Sioux: 'Surrounded'; 'Black Elk' and 'Charging Thunder'. The last we heard they were heading into town for a pint of beer and a game of darts (Or was it a game of arrows)

Sadly, 'Surrounded' died of a chest infection aged just 21 years. He died in his Tepee on Salford Quays and his body was taken to Hope Hospital in Manchester. Days later the body vanished and to this day nobody knows where it went.

Black Elk and four of his tribe were left behind in Manchester when the Show moved out of town and headed for Europe. They found themselves homeless and penniless. After wandering the streets of Manchester they worked their way across Europe and back to America. Years later Black Elk wrote a book called 'Black Elk Speaks' in it he talks about his time in Salford.

There used to be a cinema on Clowes St, Manchester. The usher was called George Edward Williams. When the cinema closed down he got a job at Belle View Circus where he looked after the elephants. George was a respected member of the community. He married Josephine an American Horse trainer from the Wild West show. Together they had children and settled down in Gorton, Manchester. Their grandchildren still live there today. Hang on a minute why am I telling you about George Edward Williams. I'll tell you why. It's because 'Charging Thunder' decided to stay on and settle in England. He changed his name to George Edward Williams. Many of Manchester's population can claim Native American ancestry. They are known as the Salford Sioux.

Wild Bill Hickok was shot and killed during a game of Poker. (Ok some of the Wild West was pretty wild)

President Theodore Roosevelt named the USA Reserve Army Cavalry 'The Rough Riders' in honour of Buffalo Bills show.

Another famous cowboy of the era, Butch Cassidy, (real name Robert Parker) had English parents His dad was from Lancashire and lived in Accrington and Preston. His mum came from Newcastle.

INTERVAL

More strange and scary entertainment

FLEA CIRCUS: Yes tiny fleas, the blood sucking dog loving pests were a huge draw in Victorian times. They would be tied to tiny pieces of wire and then forced to perform in custom built miniature circuses. You could watch them walk the highwire, sword fight, and pull miniature chariots. The owners of the flea circuses would provide magnifying glasses for paying customers.

REGURGITATORS: Egyptian born Hadji Ali would swallow live animals (small ones) and then regurgitate them, unharmed. Other acts would swallow vast amounts of water and then create elaborate fountains from their mouths. These were known as Geek acts. (So now you know where the word geek comes from) Today you can see the amazing Stevie Star perform his unique regurgitator act.

BALLOON RIDES: Performers would rise up in hot air balloons and then do a trapeze act from under the basket of the balloon. In 1852 Madame Poitevin sat on a bull which was then tied to a hot air balloon. Miraculously she survived the stunt only to later be arrested for cruelty to animals!

HUMAN CANNONBALLS: The first recorded Human Cannonball in London was 14 year old Rosa Richter, better known as Zazal. In 1877 she was sent shooting out of the cannon at the Westminster Royal Aquarium Leisure Gardens. She went on to tour with PT Barnum. In 1998 David 'Cannonball' Smith broke the world record for the human cannonball when he was shot out at a distance of 56.64 m.

STRONGMEN: In 1891 the world's greatest strongman Eugene Sandow (1867-1925) lifted a live carthorse. He is regarded as the father of bodybuilding.

Put me down you Brute!

ACT FOUR

THE GREAT

LAFAYETTE

1872-1911

This is the story of one man and his dog. Ok it's not just the story of one man and his dog. That wouldn't be much fun really, would it? Not unless you're a shepherd.   To any shepherds reading this book I do apologise. I'm sure it's lots of fun out there alone on the moors with your angry dog, chasing balls of wool........ Anyway back to the story. Like I said, it's not just about one man and his dog. This is the tale of the greatest showman of his generation (yes even greater than Houdini himself) The Great Lafayette was loved and hated in equal measure by those who knew him. Ladies and gentlemen (and shepherds) I present to you the life and death (maybe) of Master Magician and Illusionist, The Great Lafayette.

Sigmund Neuberger was born in Munich, Germany in 1872. When he was 18 yrs old his family moved to America where his father was a successful silk merchant and jeweller. However Sigmund was a natural performer and mimic. He spent his time at Vaudeville Theatres (American Music Halls) and before long he had his own act. He developed a sharp shooting act with bows and arrows (Probably influenced by Buffalo Bill) he added a quick change act and then learned a bit of conjuring.   One evening he saw a poster advertising Ching Ling Foo. (Remember Foo, he really was Chinese, not to be confused with Soo in Act 1 who was not) On seeing Foo's show the young Sigmund was awe struck. The colours and the seemingly impossible illusions gave Sigmund a hunger to become a Master Illusionist.

Sigmund became an American citizen and changed his name to The Great Lafayette. (The Great Sigmund Neuberger just doesn't sound right) He was also guilty of copying Ching Ling Foo's act. Like I said he had a great talent for mimicking! He went on a tour of American Vaudeville theatres where all his shows were sold out. But Lafayette always wanted to be greater than all the other magicians. He knew that Ling Foo was the master at Oriental magic and that he could never better him. So he changed his show and created one of the greatest magic acts that the world had ever seen.

His show was billed as a 'Carnival of Conjuring' it was split into four parts. Each section was full of vibrant colours and sounds.

Part One: Amazing feats of conjuring, including snatching live pigeons from thin air. (Makes a change from shooting them) He also had a large mechanical Teddy bear which would walk around the stage.

Part Two: Lafayette would get lumps of clay and model them into a beautiful woman which would then miraculously come to life. (I tried it, it didn't work)

Part Three: He would appear as the sinister Doctor Kremser, a hypnotic surgeon. Kremser would be decapitated (have his head cut off) and then his assistant would appear and stick it back on. (Tense, nervous headache?)

I'm over here you idiot!

Part Four: The highlight of the act would be the 'Lions Bride' Lafayette would have a real lion on stage. The lion would prowl around in its cage. The cage would be opened and the lion would pounce on a beautiful assistant. As the audience screamed in horror, the lion's skin would fall to the floor revealing 'The Great Lafayette'.

Oh yes, remember, I mentioned a dog? Well the dog also appeared in each part of the show. Her name was Beauty. Beauty was a treasured gift from Harry Houdini.

Lafayette loved Beauty more than anything else. He loved her so much that he often said he could not live without her and that when she died then his own death would follow shortly afterwards. On the door of his London House he had a sign saying 'The Home of Beauty and Lafayette'. Inside the house a sign read 'The more I see of men the more I love my dog'. If Beauty took a dislike to any guest entering the house then they were told to leave immediately and were asked not to come back. You could say that he was barking mad. (Get it........Barking mad, you know dogs and all that...Oh well)

Lafayette was a very strict man. He had few friends. In fact he kept a list of eight names who he counted as friends. These eight people were treated with great respect and Lafayette was very generous towards them. All of his staff had to salute him on sight, even in the street. He also had access to their bank accounts to check that they were not working for anybody else and none of them was allowed to drink alcohol. This very small, neat, bespectacled man who always wore expensive tailor-made suits and carried a cane was described by some people as a tyrant. Yet he paid his staff very good wages and they repaid him with great loyalty.

Anyway, back to Beauty. Beauty also had her own bathroom. Question: What do you call a dog with its own bathroom? Answer: A Shampoodle (Ignore that one, I just can't help myself). She had a jewel encrusted collar, always travelled first class and she stayed in luxury hotels. When I say travelled first class I need to explain that this would often mean travelling in a private train carriage decked out with small furniture and velvet cushions. Even Lafayette's cheque book had pictures of Beauty printed on each individual cheque.

In 1911 Lafayette was at the height of his fame. A huge Music Hall Theatre had been built in Edinburgh ready for the Royal Command Performance in the summer. It was called The Empire Palace Theatre and was one of the grandest theatres in the world. On May 1st Lafayette and Beauty along with a huge cast of assistants and animals began a two week engagement there.

Tragedy struck on the third day of the show. Without warning, Beauty had a huge fit and died. Lafayette was struck with grief. He arranged to have a proper funeral for Beauty and it was agreed that she could be buried in the Piershill Cemetery in Edinburgh, on the condition that Lafayette was also buried there when he eventually died. Beauty's funeral was arranged for Monday 10th May.

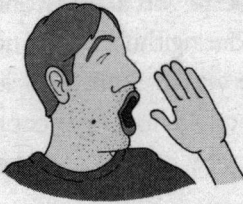

(Try this tongue twister; **Ken Dodd's dad's dogs dead.** I know it's got nothing to do with the story but try it anyway)

The night before the funeral, Lafayette arrived at the theatre to perform his show. His staff knew that he was heartbroken. He couldn't concentrate and things began to go wrong. At 11 pm a Chinese lantern on stage caught fire. The fire spread rapidly. The quick thinking stage hands dropped the fire curtain and all three thousand members of the audience left the building safely. Back stage, the fire took a fierce hold and soon the whole stage was aflame. Most of Lafayette's props were ruined. Some of the stage doors had been locked to prevent anybody spying on his well guarded illusions. This meant that the only escape route for the stage crew was a door to the rear of the building.

In all, ten people died, including a fourteen year old boy who operated the 'mechanical bear' . (His job was to climb into a bear suit and walk around mechanically) The lion used for the 'Lions Bride' also died. Lafayette had last been seen trying to rescue one of the show's horses.

His body was found on the stage next to the burnt remains of a horse. The body was taken that night and cremated. (Again)

Later that evening as the fire brigade searched through the burnt embers of the basement, one of them noticed something glistening through the ashes. It was a hand wearing Lafayette's rings.

The body previously thought to be Lafayette was actually one of his staff who acted as a body double during the show. The body in the basement was Lafayette. Or was it? Some people claim that he faked his death because he could no longer cope with the pressure of fame without Beauty by his side.

The remains of the hand were buried with Beauty. Lafayette's ashes were placed between Beauty's paws. And they were given a joint burial.

Did Lafayette really predict his own death?

Was it just a cruel coincidence?

Or did he escape the flames and use his gifts of mimicry and illusion to create another identity?

Whatever you decide, Lafayette is as much a man of mystery in death as he was in life.

Lafayette left all his money and stage props to Lalla Selbini a trick cyclist known as 'The Bathing Belle on the Bicycle'

ACT FIVE

HOUDINI

1874 - 1926

October 1926: The Super Human figure stands on stage, his midnight eyes staring menacingly at the audience. He stands almost naked except for a pair of shorts. His muscular body looks as if it has been cast in steel. Two assistants approach him cautiously, one at either side. The first assistant snaps a pair of iron handcuffs tightly onto the man's wrists and ankles. The other then begins to wrap the man in heavy chains and padlocks before hooking his bare feet to a large hoist. An audience of two thousand people gasp as the man is lifted into the air. He is now dangling upside-down, seemingly helpless without the use of his limbs. The audience look uncomfortable. Whispers skim around the theatre 'this is far too dangerous', 'somebody stop him', 'Lord have mercy'. Then a curtain is pulled back to reveal a large glass tank filled with hundreds of gallons of ice cold water. The man, still in chains and still upside-down is manoeuvred above the tank.

Before being submerged he asks the audience to hold their breath for as long as he is under the water. Slowly he is lowered down, the tank is sealed leaving only his feet sticking out. The crowd watch in anguish as his face begins to contort. His eyes look like they might shoot out of his head at any moment. Huge blue veins rise to the surface of his body and cling to his muscles, he fights frantically against the chains whilst all the time his lungs are ready to explode and splatter through his chest. The curtain is drawn over the tank. One minute passes by. Then another minute, until the audience can no longer hold on. One by one they begin to breathe again and desperately they take in air. There is now an unearthly silence. Two thousand heartbeats create an eerie soundtrack to the most death defying stunt they have ever witnessed, as they await the fate of the brave performer.

A full ten minutes later, the curtain is pulled back to reveal an empty tank. Standing triumphantly on top, free of cuffs and chains is the man of steel. This is not just any man. This is Harry Houdini. The Greatest Escape Artiste that has ever lived. Sadly, just one week later he would be dead.

Houdini was born Ehrich Weiss in Budapest, Hungary. He moved to America with his mum dad and brother when he was a toddler. Ehrich started doing card tricks at an early age. He had a double act with his brother and later on   he formed a magic act with his wife, Bess.

Harry Houdini is probably the most famous magician ever. He wasn't necessarily the greatest magician, in fact by the standards of the time he was considered to be a pretty poor magician and at the age of 27 he thought of quitting magic altogether. However he was highly original and he knew how to get publicity. The popularity of dangerous acts such as Blondin convinced Houdini that audiences liked to see performers place themselves in perilous situations. He decided to move away from conjuring and instead he became a professional 'Escape Artiste' or 'Escapologist'. (proving that he was stark raving bonkers)

An Escapologist is somebody who gets locked up with handcuffs and chains and then frees themselves without the apparent use of a key. Often Houdini would be chained up and then submerged into a water tank. He would be nailed into a coffin, locked in a milk churn, locked in a box and then thrown into a river. Each time he would free himself. He was so strong that he even offered a reward if somebody could knock him over with a punch to the stomach.

Houdini took his name from his hero, the French Illusionist Robert Houdin.

In order to get publicity for his shows, when he arrived in a new town or city he would ask the chief of police to handcuff him or lock him in a cell, then he would escape. Once during a visit to Sheffield he was locked, naked, in a police cell and his clothes were locked in the cell next door. Within five minutes Houdini walked out of the Police Station fully clothed. (I wonder if he would have been arrested if he had walked out naked and if so, how would they dare to lock him up?!)

Sir Arthur Conan Doyle the famous writer of the Sherlock Holmes stories was so impressed by Houdini's escapes that he was convinced that Houdini was able to perform real magic. Doyle thought that Houdini could turn himself into a spirit and disappear out of the chains.

Houdini did not believe in real magic, spirits or ghosts. He believed that anything supernatural should be reserved for entertainment on Halloween night and he spent a lot of time trying to prove that mediums (people who claim to speak to dead relatives) were fake.

His visit to Blackburn didn't go quite so well, a young man named William Hope Hodgson challenged Houdini to escape from a pair of handcuffs which he had brought along. Houdini realised that the handcuffs had been tampered with and he refused the challenge. Hodgson tried to embarrass Houdini by saying that he was scared, so Houdini gave in and accepted the challenge. Indeed, the cuffs had been tampered with. A stunt that would normally take him two minutes, this time,

'Let's see you get out of this one'

took two hours. Eventually he freed himself, however his wrists and arms were severely bruised and cut. Some of the audience booed him off stage and others felt sorry for him. The tension in the audience nearly turned into a riot and the police had to calm everybody down. After this eventful night, Houdini vowed never to set foot in Blackburn again, calling the Lancashire Mill Town the worst hoodlum town that he ever worked in.

William Hope Hodgson went on to become a famous writer of horror stories and science fiction. His books include: 'House on the Borderland' and 'Ghost Pirates'. He was killed in battle during the First World War.

The Blackburn incident did not put Houdini off performing. He never claimed that his escapes were real magic and part of his charm was that he used secret methods to open locks which baffled the experts.

Houdini once shared a hotel room with a man called William Bottle. Bottle was an English memory man known as Datas. His act was to let the audience ask any question and he would produce the answer from his amazing photographic memory. One night in London, Houdini and Datas got locked in their room and were late for a performance. Houdini could not open the locked door and Datas had forgotten the phone number of the hotel reception.

Houdini continued to astound audiences around the world. In order to gain more publicity he came up with even more death defying stunts. In 1910 he became the first person to fly a powered aircraft over Australia.

He also realised that people were taking notice of moving pictures. By the early 1900's the cinema was becoming just as popular as live theatre. Houdini became an actor and stared in a series of films called 'The Master Mystery'. Houdini had become the first movie 'Action Hero'.

Did you know that any act that has appeared just once on Britain's Got Talent will have been seen by more people than Houdini performed to in his entire lifetime?

By 1925 Houdini was probably the most famous performer in the world. He was getting tired of travelling the globe (try explaining all those handcuffs and chains to the customs officers) and he decided to put on some shows in the USA and Canada. In October 1926 he visited a college in Montreal, Canada to give a lecture on magic. He was in his dressing room when three college students knocked on his door. One of the students was aware of the reward on offer for punching Houdini in the stomach. He suddenly, without warning, began to throw punches to Houdini's stomach.

Houdini was not prepared for the assault and he did not have time to tense his muscles. However he stood up to the challenge and the students left the room. Houdini was shaken. He began to get stomach pains which were so bad he developed a fever. His wife, Bess, asked him to cancel all his shows and to see a doctor. Houdini did not want to let his audience down. He went on stage and completed his act even though he was in immense pain. After the show he was rushed to hospital. He died on Sunday 31st October, Halloween night.

Before he died he gave Bess a secret word. He said that if mediums are genuine then one of them will pass on this word. Bess never received the message from Houdini.

Houdini's death was not caused by the punch to the stomach. An inquiry showed that he was suffering from an inflamed appendix.

ACT SIX

BLONDIN

1824 - 1897

Ok, remember the introduction, our mate, Jean Francois Gravolet. (That's Charles Blondin to his fans) was about to walk across a tightrope which was 50m above the Niagara River. Oh yes and he was wearing stilts. He was also wearing a leotard, you know, one of those things your little sister wears for ballet lessons.

They are called Leotards because they were designed by the famous French Trapeze Artiste, Jules Leotard. He would perform his act above the audience without a safety net, swinging from rope to rope whilst doing somersaults. He died aged 28 from Smallpox.

One of the most famous trapeze acts of the day was Lulu 'The Beautiful Girl Aerialist' the petite blonde would perform triple somersaults in mid air. It was only in her later years that Lulu was exposed as being a man, born El Nino Farini in 1855.

You forgot to wash your hands!

Anyway, back to Blondin's tightrope across the Niagara Falls.....................................

The crowd stare up at Blondin. He moves his right stilt forward and then gently steps onto the rope. He looks around at the crowd with an arrogance that holds their attention. Yes Blondin is a huge attraction and he knows it, he loves it, he loves the crowd and he loves himself, he is definitely a bit of a bighead.

He holds his position for a short while in order to maximise the tension, then slowly he lifts his left stilt on to the rope. A wild cheer erupts. They know that one slight mistake will see the big headed ....I mean, Blondin crash into the swirling water and jagged rocks below. The only outcome will be certain death.

This time he looks nervous. The thing is, Blondin was a Master of his Art and nerves didn't really have any effect on him. The nervous look was just part of his image. Blondin was a true showman. (Whilst crossing a tightrope he would often pretend to trip up and almost fall. This kept the audience coming back for more).

He edges out onto the rope which stretches across the river for over 300 metres. As he reaches the middle he wobbles, stops to catch his breath and then continues. By the time he reaches the other side the crowd are going wild. Ever the showman, he offers to give a piggy back to a waiting journalist. The sensible man refuses and Blondin returns triumphantly to the other side.

But why I hear you ask, did he cross the river on stilts? Why didn't he just walk across the rope on foot? Surely that's enough to attract a crowd? OK I'll let you into a secret. This was not the first time that Blondin had crossed the Niagara. His first crossing, in fact, the first ever historic crossing was a year earlier in 1859.

Blondin (He got his name because of his long blonde hair) was born in France. As a five year old child his father had taken him to see a circus. He was so amazed by the tightrope act that when he got home he tied a rope between two chairs and began to practice. (Do Not Try this at home. I repeat Do Not Try this at home, not even on your Grandmas washing line; she was bad enough when you asked her what it was like before TV was invented!!)

By the age of six, he was being billed as the 'The Little Wonder'. His father who was a gymnast (I wonder what acrobats and gymnasts wore before Leotard invented the leotard) encouraged Blondin to perform. He sent the young boy to a special school for acrobats. Sadly Blondin Senior, who had encouraged and nurtured his sons talent, died when Blondin was just nine years old.

He had to grow up fast. He needed to earn money to survive. A circus company heard about him and offered him a job. Before long he was in New York performing in PT Barnum's 'Greatest Show on Earth'. He continued to work as a circus performer and for a number of years he toured America and

Canada. In 1858 the circus arrived at Niagara Falls. The 34 year old Blondin was awestruck. The sheer beauty and power of the falls cast a spell over him. From that day on he made it his mission to conquer the Niagara River by tightrope.

Other daredevils at Niagara include Englishman Captain Matthew Webb. In 1883 he attempted to swim across the rapids but was dragged into a whirlpool to his death. (ask your grandma about Captain Webb Matches)

In 1901 school teacher Annie Edson Taylor climbed into a barrel and then took the scariest ride of her life. She became the first person to survive the almost suicidal feat of going over the falls in a wooden barrel. Few people have survived to tell the tale.

Just one year later on June 30th 1859 Blondin achieved his ambition. In fact he crossed the river on 17 more occasions. In order to keep attracting the huge crowds each crossing was done a little differently. So, you already know about the stilts. Surely it doesn't get any crazier than that does it? Well make up your own mind:

He crossed blindfolded..............

He crossed whilst carrying his manager on his back. (Not sure who is the braver, Blondin or his manager)..................

He crossed whilst pushing a wheelbarrow.................

He carried a chair with him and balanced on it in the middle of the rope..............

He once actually stopped in the middle and cooked an omelette. He then lowered a rope down to the spectators on the 'Maid of the Mist' who tied a bottle of water onto it so he could wash the omelette down.................

The first woman to tightrope across the Niagara was the Italian Maria Spelterini in 1876. She once even crossed wearing handcuffs and manacles around her ankles. (I wonder if Houdini had heard about this.)

In 1867, Selena Powell, billed as the female Blondin, fell to her death from a 10m high tightrope during a performance in Aston, Birmingham.

Because of these amazing feats of daring, Blondin became World Famous. He also became a very wealthy man. He moved to England and settled in Ealing, London. He was billed as Blondin 'The Hero of Niagara' and he would have a huge picture of the falls as a backdrop to his act.

His feats of daring became even more extreme. He began to tightrope whilst in a sack. He even performed summersaults on the rope whist wearing stilts.

However, one night in Liverpool, Blondin proved that he was human after all. Yes, the incredible man with the nerves of steel decided to put a lion (a real one with large teeth and razor sharp paws) into a wheelbarrow. He began to push the bewildered wild animal across the rope. Everything was going smoothly until half way across; the wheelbarrow got snagged on a supporting rope. Blondin and the lion were stuck 20 metres above the auditorium without a safety net.

Nice kitty !

The lion began to roar and attempted to free itself from the wheelbarrow. The audience fled in panic. Fortunately Blondin had the sense to strap the lion in before attempting the stunt. Eventually he managed to free the wheelbarrow and both of them made it across safely. The news of this near miss only made him even more famous and soon he was booked to perform at Crystal Palace. He again used the wheelbarrow, only this time, inside, was his five year old daughter, Adele. Blondin wheeled her across the rope and then Adele, in true Blondin showmanship fashion, showered the audience with flower petals.

This must have been an astonishing sight. Not surprisingly many of the audience and reporters, who witnessed this amazing feat, were concerned for the welfare of Adele. They were right to be concerned. If it had gone wrong, Adele would have fallen 30 metres onto a concrete floor. (Ouch).....**Splats entertainment!**

Blondin continued to perform into his old age. His popularity never faded and his arrogance was really just part of his theatrical image. Blondin was one of the Greatest Showmen who ever lived. He died peacefully in his sleep in 1897 at the age of 75.

Frenchman Philippe Petit is sometimes known as the new Blondin. In 1974 he tight roped between the ill fated Twin Towers in New York at a height of 417 metres. The police officers, who arrested him at the scene, reported that he was dancing on the rope. In 1986 he paid tribute to Blondin by re-enacting the Niagara crossings.

ACT SEVEN

P T BARNUM

1810 - 1891

The Hull of the huge cargo ship pokes through the eerie Victorian smog heading for the East London Tobacco Docks. Its exhausted crew have just arrived from the East Indies. They stand on the decks peering at the gas lit windows in the distance and listen to the singing and laughter drifting out of the taverns and Inns which line the cobbled streets. Thousands of sacks, full of spices and huge vats of exotic oils are packed tightly in the hold of the ship along with crates of tea and coffee beans.

A well dressed gentleman named Charles Jamarach steps out of the shadows and approaches the ship. He has been waiting for a special consignment. His Emporium (that's shop to you) is running low on stock and one of his best customers, PT Barnum has placed a huge order. A jumbo sized order.

Jamarach walks up the gangplank and then climbs down into the bowels of the huge vessel. The sweet smells of spice, oil, tea and coffee are beaten back mercilessly by the stench of Jamarach's load. (No he hasn't just flushed and left the door open) Jamarach deals in wild animals. He is the owner of The Wild Beast Depot on Ratcliffe Highway, London. Yes believe it or not you could walk in and buy a giraffe if you really wanted to. (Jamarach kept hundreds of caged animals in his Emporium)

TYPICAL PRICE LIST FROM THE WILD BEAST DEPOT

**TIGER: £200; LION £70; ELEPHANT: FROM £300;
BARBARY APE: £4; RHINO: £600**

Jamarach is at the Docks to collect a consignment of Elephants, Tigers, Lions, Crocodiles, Rhinos, Leopards and nearly any other dangerous animal you can think of. (Yes even more dangerous than a Chav's Pit Bull)

In 1857, one of Jamarach's Tigers escaped from a packing crate on the Docks. Everybody fled in terror apart from an eight year old boy named John Wade who gently walked up to the ferocious beast and patted it on the nose. In return the Tiger belted him across the head with its giant paw and carried him off down a back alley hoping for a spot of lunch. Legend has it that Jamarach prized the boy from the Jaws of the tiger and saved him from certain death. There is a statue dedicated to the incident on Wapping Docks, London.

Another version of the story says that a Docker tried to save the boy. He attacked the tiger with a crowbar and instead of hitting the tiger the crowbar came down on Johns head, crushing his skull.

OK so what has this got to do with entertainment I hear you ask and why are you going on about a strange bloke who sells wild beasts for living? Well remember I said that Jamarach had a jumbo sized order. Barnum is waiting for an Elephant to exhibit in his show.

PT Barnum was born in Bethel Connecticut on July 5th 1810. He started out as an entertainer appearing with 'Barnum's Grand Scientific and Musical Theatre'. He soon realised that there was more money to be earned by promoting shows than there was by appearing in them. (Simon Cowell has probably earned more money than all of his acts put together)

Barnum was a true entrepreneur. He became a master of publicity. He knew that to keep the crowds coming back for more then he needed to make sure that they had something better and different to come back to. His motto was:

'Every crowd has a silver lining'

He always booked the most popular or most unusual acts of the day.

His most famous act was General Tom Thumb. Tom Thumb was born Charles Sherwood Stratton in 1838. He also hailed from Connecticut and was a distant relative of Barnum. He stopped growing at the age of six months and for most of his career he stood just 64cm tall. Barnum taught him to sing and dance and he also dressed him in a variety of costumes to the amusement of the massive crowds who paid to see him.

Barnum took Tom Thumb to England where he performed for Queen Victoria. The Queen was very amused. This added to Stratton's fame and in turn fattened Barnum's wallet. By this time Barnum owned museums, theatres, circuses and other travelling shows, he even had his own railroad (Richard Branson springs to mind)

It was during another visit to London to perform for Queen Victoria that Barnum heard about Jumbo the Elephant. Jumbo was the most popular attraction at London Zoo and he was so friendly he would give rides to children on his huge back. Barnum wanted to buy Jumbo and take him to America to be part of his huge spectacular show billed as Barnum and Bailey's 'The Greatest Show on Earth'. (Remember, it's the show in which Blondin appeared in). He also wanted to buy the birthplace of William Shakespeare. At the time, Shakespeare's House in Stratford upon Avon was a little bit run down and Barnum could see the potential to dismantle it and build it again so that American audiences could see it for themselves.

In 1967, American, Robert McCulloch bought the 1831 London Bridge and dismantled it brick by brick. He had it sent over to America. Unfortunately, he thought he was buying Tower Bridge. He was very disappointed to see the plain old boring London Bridge. It now stands near to the Colorado River.

Barnum placed an order with Jamarach. He promised to pay him thousands of pounds to have 18 elephants shipped to America, with one condition. One of the elephants must be the famous Jumbo. (Jumbo got his name from the African word for hello which is Jambo) Many people were outraged. 100,000 children signed a petition to keep Jumbo at London Zoo. It was the same in Stratford. Thousands of people protested that Shakespeare's House was part of England's heritage. The extremely clever Barnum said that he would stop his interest in Shakespeare's House if he could buy Jumbo. It was elephant loving children versus Shakespeare loving adults. Barnum got his own way. (I mean, really, who is going to listen to 100,000 moaning kids.) Only joking. No really I am. Bring back Jumbo, that's what I say. Well actually we can't bring him back because he's no longer with us. But if he was, I'd keep Jumbo and send the house. Honest.

In 1882 Jumbo set off for America to join Tom Thumb in 'The Greatest Show on Earth'.

One year later Charles Stratton aged only 45, died after collapsing at home. 10,000 people attended his funeral. Barnum bought a small elephant as a new companion for Jumbo. Because of its size he called it Tom Thumb in honour of Stratton. The show moved by train from city to city. In 1885, the train pulled into Ontario, Canada, and as was usual, all the animals were let out to get air and stretch their legs. Tom Thumb (The small elephant) ran towards an oncoming train. Jumbo spotted this and he bravely pushed the young elephant out of danger. Sadly Jumbo could not save himself and the train smashed into him. He died on the spot.

Entertaining the masses was Barnum's passion. He knew that if the crowd did not get their money's worth then they wouldn't come back. It's the same today.

All of these amazing people spent their lives touring the world and bringing joy to millions of people. Live entertainers are still out there. Turn off the telly and go out and see them. Who knows? Maybe you will become one. Try some of the tricks on the next few pages.

THE 1089 PREDICTION

Ask somebody for a three figure number e.g. 274 or 263 etc.

Once you have the number reverse it and take away the smallest from the largest.

Example.

274 reversed is 472. Take away the smallest from the largest 472 minus 274 is 198.

Once you have your answer reverse the numbers again and this time add them together. 198 reversed is 891. 891 plus 198 is 1089

If you follow this procedure the answer will always be 1089. However there are a few rules. Don't use noughts and don't use duplicate numbers. E.g. 446 or 522 etc.

So make sure that the three digit number contains three different numbers and no noughts.

To make this a truly amazing trick find a book that has a page 10 that has at least eight lines down and on the eighth line has nine words across. Write the ninth word on a piece of paper and seal it in an envelope. Away you go.

Give the envelope to a member of the audience (one of your mates)

Do the maths till you get your answer 1089

Hand out the book

Tell somebody to go to page 10, count 8 lines down and 9 words across.

Ask them to say the word. Then get them to open the envelope and read out the prediction. It works every time.

Think of a number between one and nine

Multiply it by nine

Add the two digits together eg if you thought of three then multiplied by nine it will be 27. Add together 2 and 7. If you initially thought of the number 1 then multiplied by 9 you will already only have one digit.

Then subtract 5

Correlate your new number to a letter of the alphabet.
Eg. 1 is A, 2 is B etc.

Think of a country which begins with your letter

Then with the second letter of your country think of a zoo animal

Finally what is the common colour of the animal

TURN OVER THE PAGE TO SEE IF I WAS RIGHT.

FAMILY PREDICTION

Make sure that the audience do this on paper or in their head. You only want the final three digit number.

Ask somebody to think of how many brothers they have

Double it

Add three

Times by five

Add the number of sisters they have to the result of the previous questions.

Multiply by 10

Add the number of living grandparents

Subtract 150.

Ask them to tell you the answer.

If the steps have been followed correctly the first digit of the result will be the number of brothers they have. The second digit the number of sisters they have and the last digit the number of living grandparents.

These are just three simple but effective tricks. Play about with them and add your own patter. (Stories and jokes) Magic like most performance is about presentation.

oooooooooooooooooo THAT'S ENTERTAINMENT.

Please make sure that you have all your belongings with you (i-pod, bar of chocolate) as you leave the auditorium. (Your classroom or bedroom)   I am currently rehearsing my next book and I look forward to presenting you with the amazing 'Terrifyingly Criminal'

Goodnight.

Vote for your favourite Act at www.andywinters.co.uk

Andy Winters ran away from the circus to become a teacher. He has travelled the world as one half of the magic/variety act 'The Incredible Blood Brothers' (His stage name is Cornelius Gold) Andy loves films, books, music and sport, he reckons that he's a pretty good pool player. He currently works within the Youth Justice System and he has created a number of educational resources. He travels to schools, libraries, festivals and youth centres throughout the country with his unique and entertaining author visit/literacy sessions.

Al Jacques is a friendly Yorkshire man. He graduated from Nottingham Trent University with a degree in graphic design and illustration. He has an obsession with line and colour and Yorkshire pudding.